INTRODUC

It was the Duke of York, later King Geoı
speech to the Royal Academy in 1924 tha. ... ...
villages with carved or painted name signs ought to be revived. By
then, the Kent village of Biddenden had already won a Daily Mail
Competition in 1920 for its sign featuring the two Biddenden Maids on
what remains probably the best-known of all the county's village signs.
Several villages celebrated the Coronation of Queen Elizabeth II in
1953 with specially designed signs and more followed.

Although Kent lagged behind some other counties, it has caught up
rapidly in recent years and an outbreak of 'Millennium' signs has meant
that about half of all the county's villages are now identified with
attractive signs of their own. Some of the earlier ones have been
replaced by new ones; some have been removed completely; and
several more villages have plans to install a sign in the near future.

This selection of some of the most distinctive and interesting village
signs in Kent brings the county into line with other counties that have
already had selections of their village signs published and it includes
many that were illustrated in the weekly series published by the Kent
Messenger in 2001/2 by staff photographers. They all have something
to say about the villages they represent, many of which, because of
Kent's pre-eminent role in British history, are heirs to some of the
country's most colourful relics of history and legend.

Alan Bignell 2004.

APPLEDORE

Appledore was one of several Kent villages that treated themselves to a village sign to mark the millennium. This one is an eye-catching design, with an apple tree fretted in painted ironwork within a slightly unusually shield-shaped metal frame topped with nicely restrained wrought ironwork. The name of the village is in gold lettering across the top of the shield and the tree seems to grow out of the solid black ground on which is written the date, 2000 AD.

Once, the village was an important riverside trading and ship building port but it declined after the River Rother changed its course in 1286, although until the end of the 19th century it still exercised its right, granted by Edward III in 1359, to hold a weekly market and an annual January fair.

In 1804-7 the Royal Military Canal was dug as one of the defences against a threatened French invasion. It was never put to the test, enabling the Kent cleric and wit Richard Barham, author of The Ingoldsby Legends, to point out that "although Napoleon's armies crossed the Rhine and the Rhone and other insignificant currents, they never did pass Mr Pitt's Military Canal."

The canal-side military road improved Appledore's links with both Hythe and Rye and proved to be of great benefit in draining the swampy, fever-ridden area and beginning the environmental improvement that made the village the very pleasant place it is today.

BARHAM

Larger signs than Barham's are more usually supported on a single upright beam, but this one is framed by two uprights and a substantial lintel, so that it looks a bit like a wooden guillotine, standing on the village green beside the road through the village, poised to do its fatal duty.

The sign itself is shield-shaped and painted with three bears on white grounds, two above and one below a red band bearing two choughs (birds of the crow family) separated by a fleur de lys, a reference to the FitzUrse family who once owned Barham Court (the bears) and Canterbury (the choughs). A FitzUrse was one of the knights who, believing they were carrying out the wishes of the king, murdered Archbishop Thomas Becket in Canterbury Cathedral in 1170.

Below the shield, the name of the village is carved into a label above the daintily shaped bottom of the sign.

An unique feature is the little mouse carved into the upright woodwork, the signature of the craftsman who made it, known locally as Mousey.

Barham is an attractive and historic village of mainly red brick houses situated between the A2 and the B2065, with a long street overlooked by the slender green copper spire of the 13th century church of St John the Baptist.

BARMING

Barming's village sign stands on the grass verge beside the Maidstone-Tonbridge road (A26) at the western end of the village.

It bears a cross of foliated brambles, a reminder that an early form of the village name signified a settlement in a bramble clearing. The White Horse of Kent forms the centrepiece of the cross.

In the top left quarter is an open book inscribed with the date 1080 above the Domesday spelling of the village name, Bermelie. Top right is a depiction of St Margaret's Church; bottom left, a sprig of oak leaves with acorns illustrative of the wooded nature of the area; and, bottom right, Barming's old wooden St Helen's Bridge (now replaced), topped by three fruit trees representing the wealth of orchards that once distinguished the entire Medway Valley.

The bridge was the only wooden bridge across the River Medway and was the scene of a dramatic accident in April 1914 when it collapsed under the weight of a traction engine with a four-man crew. Luckily, no-one was badly hurt and the vehicle was later recovered.

Barming Heath was crossed by Parliamentarians before the Civil War Battle of Maidstone in 1648 and in 1828 the county asylum, which became Oakwood psychiatric hospital, was built there. That is now closed and the site is being redeveloped with houses.

Hermitage Lane, which takes its name from a 15th century woodland chapel, passes Maidstone District General Hospital and Barming railway station on its way to the neighbouring parish of Aylesford.

BEARSTED

The village sign on The Green at Bearsted depicts a top-hatted cricketer defending his wicket and is a memorial to the 19th century Kent cricketer, Alfred ('Mighty') Mynn, who once played on this same village green.

Mynn was born in 1807 the son of a gentleman farmer in Goudhurst. Several generations of his family earned reputations for exceptional height and strength and Alfred himself grew to top six feet and weigh 18 stone.

He trained as an architect but after the family moved to Harrietsham in 1825 young Mynn became so hooked on the game of cricket that he neglected his business for the game to which he devoted most of his life and almost all his money. With the financial support of friends, he became the greatest all-rounder the game had ever had.

He earned the title of The Lion of Kent in 1832 when he became the county single wicket champion. In that same year, he first played at Lords and from then on he played regularly for Kent until 1854 and then less regularly until 1860. In the first Canterbury Cricket Week Kent v England game in 1842 he defended his wicket for most of one day and during his career Kent became the most successful cricketing county in England.

Mynn, who lived at Chrismill House in Bearsted, once hit the ball from the middle of Bearsted Green over some brewery buildings and gardens into a field beyond.

Later, he lived at Mount Pleasant in nearby Ware Street but he died in London in 1861, aged 54 and was buried in Thurnham churchyard.

BENEDEN

Benenden has bequeathed some famous cricketing names to Kent, and two of them are portrayed on the sign which stands on the green beside the A2086, opposite a building that was, in 1609, the Edmund Gibbon School, and between the William IV and The Bull public houses.

It is a two-sided sign, sturdily framed in timber with a small wrought iron decoration on the top. On one side is a portrait of a top-hatted, white-garbed wicket-keeper, identified as Edward G (Gower) Wenman, who was born in the village in 1803. A wheelwright by trade, he became a noted cricketer who first played at Lords for Kent against Marylebone in 1828. The other side of the sign depicts the no less famous Richard Mills, here seen, similarly dressed and leaning on his bat beside a wicket. In 1834, these two stalwarts played a double wicket game at Wittersham against an eleven from the Isle of Oxney (part of Romney Marsh) and knocked up 198 runs between them while their opponents could only reply with 132.

The Edmund Gibbon who founded the school that still bears his name, although it is no longer a school, was a member of the family of that Gibbon who is remembered as the author of his "Rise and Fall of the Roman Empire" and the village is probably best-known today for the school at which Princess Anne, the Princess Royal, was a pupil.

BETHERSDEN

This unusual circular sign, with the name of the village arcing over the top, has a colourful village scene centred upon St Margaret's Church for its centre piece, bordered with symbols illustrating features characteristic of the village.

In the twelve o'clock position a pair of oast kilns recall the importance of hop farming until the 1970s and other symbols include an anvil (a reminder that Bethersden has a long tradition of being part of the historic Wealden iron industry), shears (representing the importance of local sheep farming), a pig (hinting at the 11th century name of Beadericesdenne, meaning woodland where swine are pastured), and an open book in memory of the 17th century Cavalier poet Richard Lovelace who owned land in Bethersden and, while imprisoned in 1642 for his support of the Kent petition, wrote the poem "To Althea, from Prison" with the memorable opening lines: "Stone walls do not a prison make, Nor iron bars a cage...." Part of Bethersden church is known as the Lovelace Chapel.

A plate fixed to the sign's very substantial upright, tells readers that the material used in making the sign includes iron, oak and a limestone known as Bethersden marble, and that beneath the base is buried a time capsule to be opened no sooner than 2100 AD.

The "marble" referred to was formed from fossilised shells of freshwater snails and although it is no longer quarried it is still to be found in a number of Kent churches and elsewhere.

BIDDENDEN

This must surely be the best-known and most-photographed - as well as being one of the earliest - village signs in Kent. Although the overall design remains the same, there have been a number of changes since the first one won a special award in a Daily Mail competition in 1920, not least to the dress style of the celebrated Biddenden Maids who are featured on it. The post on which it stands is indisputably the most-decorated of that of any village sign in the county.

The Maids, Mary and Eliza Chulkhurst, were England's first recorded Siamese twins, and they lived together, in a very literal sense, joined at the shoulder and the hip, for more than 30 years. They were the daughters of a prosperous local farmer, born about 1100 and when one of them fell ill and died, the other refused the surgery that could have separated them and died a few hours later, fulfilling her own wish that they should leave the world as they had entered it, together.

They left 18 acres of land, later known as The Bread and Cheese Lands, to the parish to pay for a dole of bread, cheese and beer to be distributed to the local poor every Easter. The distribution took place inside the church until 1682, when the rector reported to the Archbishop that the custom was being continued "amid much disorder and indecency" and the beer handout was discontinued. Today, the dole is perpetuated by biscuits imprinted with a representation of the twins.

BILSINGTON

Bilsington overlooks the Royal Military Canal and Romney Marsh beyond it, on the B2067, south of Ashford. This two-sided wrought iron framed sign at the crossroads outside the White Horse public house has a different illustration on each side, each with the Kent badge, the White Horse on a red shield, in the top right-hand corner.

On one side, a clerical gentleman makes a somewhat oblique reference to the former Bilsington Priory, now a private house, and he stands beside a bell hanging in a lychgate, a reference to the local church of St Peter and St Paul which does, in fact, have its bell hanging in a lychgate.

On the other side, the sign shows the Cosway obelisk, a local landmark built by local people to the memory of William Cosway, a baker's son who became the owner of the Priory during the 19th century and bought the manor of Bilsington in 1825. He was at one time secretary to Vice-Admiral Collingwood and was aboard the Royal Sovereign at the Battle of Trafalgar, but he was probably never called upon to fulfil the traditional obligations that went with ownership of the manor, of carrying the last dish of the second course to the king's table, and presenting the monarch with three maple cups at a coronation.

He was knighted in 1829 but at the age of 50 he was killed when he was thrown from the coach in which he was travelling from London to Brighton.

BIRLING

Travellers along the M20 and A20 might make the journey between London and the Channel coast without ever knowing they were bypassing the coyly pleasant little village of Birling, which tucks itself into the lower slopes of the North Downs as though in retirement from the hurly-burly of modern life.

But a century ago, its main street was part of the highway between the industrial riverside at Snodland and the market town of West Malling, and long before that it was on the route of pilgrims travelling to Rochester, Boxley and Canterbury.

The wrought iron village sign stands near the church and the war memorial. It was made by village blacksmith Len Kilner and, unlike many other signs, it is "see-through", the only background being the sky behind it.

The square sign is divided vertically and with top and bottom separated by a thin metal chevron. At the bottom, the Nevill bull, symbol of the aristocratic family whose 700 year association with the village made an enduring impact, confronts the Kent horse.

Above these two ancient heraldic animals, two pilgrims caper joyfully, enjoying a respite from their travels, and across the top of the sign is the name of the village. The whole is embellished with wrought iron scrollwork around the frame.

The sign, which was instigated by Birling Village Society, stands on a timber upright that was donated by local fencing contractor Bill Palmer.

BOBBING

The 20th century did not treat the village of Bobbing very well. First, it poured increasingly heavy traffic through it on the way from Sheerness and the Isle of Sheppey to the A2 and, later, the M2, then it wrapped it around with new roads until it was pretty well indistinguishable. Perhaps its residents prefer it that way.

The village sign stands on a small grassed area at the Key Street junction and acknowledges the fact with a large key nestling on a foreground of oak leaves and acorns beyond which is the village church of St Bartholomew. The domed-topped sign is supported by two metal columns topped with acorns, the whole standing on a sturdy timber upright.

The church was built during the 14th century, but although William the Conqueror's bureaucrats seem to have overlooked it when they were compiling his Domesday Survey during the 11th century, the village was certainly there then. Its name is of pre-Conquest Saxon origin, and tells us that this was the chosen settlement of Bobba's people.

Bobbing's chief claim to historical notoriety is as the home of the unscrupulous Titus Oates who, in 1678, stirred up a national hornets' nest by inventing a Romish plot to murder Charles II, and falsely accusing a number of Catholics of implication. His perjury was discovered and he was punished by a spell in the pillory, a public whipping through the streets of London and imprisonment for life, although four years later, in 1689, he was pardoned and pensioned off.

BONNINGTON

This rather colourful, wooden-framed sign depicts two ancient warriors standing in the shade of the Bonnington Oak which, according to local lore, was where the former Leet Court was held during the Middle Ages. The name of the village is prominently displayed across the bottom.

When the author Ford Madox Ford lived in the village briefly in the 1890s he described it as a scattered, little-populated village in the south of England. More precisely, it is at the junction of the B2069 with the B2067, south of Ashford and about a mile east of Bilsington aforementioned.

Former owners of Bonnington manor have included the Knights Templar, suppressed by Edward II early in the 14th century, the Knights Hospitaller, in their turn suppressed by Henry VIII in the mid-16th century, and by Sir James Hale, who was the only judge who refused to sign the Instrument legitimising Lady Jane Gray as Queen.

The church, which is said to be the oldest on Romney Marsh, is some little distance from the present village centre, and is dedicated, somewhat oddly, to St Rumwold, the child-saint who is reputed to have preached a sermon to his parents on his second day, before he died on his third day, bequeathing to the 19th century Rev Richard Barham the inspiration for his Lay of St Rumwold (or The Blasphemer's Warning), one of his delightfully tongue-in-cheek Ingoldsby Legends.

BORDEN

The visitor to Borden, just south-west of Sittingbourne, who looks up at the village sign which stands in front of the is looking at a reflection of the village itself.

The timber-framed sign, mounted on a slim metal pole, is painted with a scene depicting the main road through the village, with the pub on one side, houses on the other and the church, St Peter and St Paul's, in the centre, where the road bends to leave the village. The name, Borden, is in bold gold-coloured lettering on a green ground across the bottom of the picture.

It sums up the village very adequately and charmingly. Although Borden has some picturesque architectural features, it does not revel in any major topographical details or contributions to Kent history. It has kept itself pretty much to itself since the parish was founded in 1160, when the first vicar was appointed, although it is possible that Romans worshipped in a temple on the site of the present church. The village took its name from the Borden family, which later settled in North America.

During the 17th century, Borden bellfounders Henry and John Wilnar are thought to have had a casting pit in Boundary Field, which gave rise to the local story that the Devil once threw one of the church bells from the tower into the field, leaving a hollow there.

BOUGHTON MONCHELSEA

The village sign at Boughton Monchelsea was designed and painted by local resident and nationally renowned artist Graham Clarke and mounted by local blacksmith Stuart Potter. It shows a typically Graham Clarke rustic scene, with a hilltop church, a single deer to represent the herd of fallow deer that were a feature of Robert Rudston's 16th century Monchelsea Place deer park for 300 years, a white cowled oast house and a traditional cottage separated by stylised fruit and other trees. The foreground is held by a smocked shepherd on one side and a pick-carrying quarryman on the other, symbolising the two local industries, fruit farming and stone quarrying, and the name of the village is painted on scrolls above and below the scene.

For most of 2,000 years ragstone was quarried at Boughton and used for major buildings throughout Kent and beyond. Westminster Abbey was one of many London landmark buildings for which stone from the Boughton quarries was used. Some of the 7,000 cannon balls supplied by the quarries to Henry V may have contributed to his victory at Agincourt in 1415 and damage caused to the Houses of Parliament in the London Blitz of 1940 was repaired with Boughton ragstone.

Quarrying declined in the 1930s and now Boughton's main claim to fame is the 15th century lychgate of St Peter's Church, said to be one of the oldest in England.

BOXLEY

Most village signs have illustrations on both sides; sometimes, a different one on each side. Boxley, however, decided that only people leaving The King's Arms or approaching the church needed to be able to see its sign, so it illustrated one side only.

It has the appearance of a wooden-framed window giving a view over the local scene, with a foreground white horse, coated and bridled, turning its head away to look at the distant church over the wayside sign displaying the name of the village. A notice explains that the art work was by Jonathan Catt and that the sign was provided by Boxley Parish Council, 2000.

Boxley village, just north of Maidstone and saddling the North Downs where they are crossed by the old Roman road from Rochester through The Weald, is no longer one of Kent's major tourist attractions, as it was in the Middle Ages, when it was a place of pilgrimage in itself and a "must see" for pilgrims on their way to Canterbury. The Cistercian abbey that was founded in 1145 became first famous and later infamous for its miraculous (mechanical) images of Christ and St Rumwold. Little remains today apart from the 200 feet long 13th century tithe barn.

The cobbled path that leads up to the Church of St Mary and All Saints, past the village sign, may actually be part of the Roman road and the church itself may have been built, in about 1100, on the site of a Romano-British chapel.

BRASTED

Brasted, in the Holmesdale Valley west of Sevenoaks, exhibits its village sign on the little village green beside the main A25 road. A helpful plate fixed to the supporting upright explains that the foreground figure is a mediaeval Archbishop of Canterbury, standing in and blessing the garden of Brasted, a reference to the fact that Brasted, like neighbouring Sundridge and Chevening, are known as the Archbishop's Garden and the living is still in his gift.

The sign also shows Brasted church, the river Darent and its bridges, with the North Downs in the background and the Pilgrims' Way leading to the distant towers of Canterbury.

The armorial shield, surrounded by the Garter Ribbon, is that of the 7th Earl Stanhope, who was Lord of the Manor of Brasted in 1951.

Brasted Place is one of only two houses in Kent designed by Robert Adam. Built in 1784 for John Turton, George III's physician, it became the home of Prince Louis Napoleon, from where he set out, in 1840, on an ill-fated adventure to restore the Napoleonic dynasty. He was arrested as soon as he landed in France, imprisoned, and only later assumed the restored title of Emperor Napoleon III through more constitutional means.

BREDGAR

The apparent simplicity of the pictorial design of Bredgar's village sign, executed entirely in black metal silhouette, is very attractively balanced by the detail it contains. A house flanked by bare-branched trees is reflected in the pond which is a feature of the village, just across the road from where the sign stands, at the junction of Gore Road with Primrose Lane, opposite the war memorial.

The skeletal name of the village underlines the pictorial part of the sign, which is topped by scrolled ironwork supporting the WI monogram, an acknowledgment that the sign was, as is explained on the metal plaque on the timber upright, given to the village by Bredgar WI to commemorate its Golden Jubilee Year in 1972.

The sign was designed by Norman Hepple, RA and made by D L Sattin of Teynham.

Bredgar is a pleasant little Downland village clustered around the flint church of St John the Baptist, which has stood for about 500 years, although there has been a church at Bredgar certainly since the 11th century and possibly longer. Behind trees near the pond lies the College, founded by Robert de Bradegar in 1393, which is now a private house.

Bredgar earned itself a mention in the Kentish Gazette in July 1786, when the paper reported that a Leeds (near Maidstone) shoemaker, Mr Cary, was stopped by footpads on his way home from a feast at Bredgar and robbed of eight guineas, 15 shillings and sixpence (about £9.17p today). Not a good end to a jolly evening.

BREDHURST

Some of Kent's North Downs villages seem to delight in hiding away from travellers who want to seek them out and few do it more successfully than Bredhurst, in spite of having the M2 virtually on its doorstep, although inaccessible from the village. It lies amid a tangle of ill-signed lanes, roughly between Rainham (west of Sittingbourne) and Maidstone and even its villagers would not claim it as one of the county's showpiece villages.

Nevertheless, it does have a village sign, which stands beside The Bell inn, depicting a rather charmingly bucolic scene in which a be-ribboned maypole stands among the flowers alongside a path leading to the somewhat austere-looking church, St Peter's. The illustration is framed on two sides by pinnacled columns and supported on the upright by strap and hoop brackets. The name of the village is enscrolled across the bottom.

The typically Downland flint church in reality huddles among woodland a little aside from its congregation, where its 13th century origins have been overlaid with 19th century additions that include a little bellcote housing two bells.

One 16th century owner of the manor left it to her son with instructions that he should hold "a drinking" in the village on All Saints Day and the tradition continued until the 19th century when it was allowed to lapse, although no doubt The Bell does its best to perpetuate a 21st century equivalent.

BRENCHLEY

Brenchley is one of Kent's showpiece villages. Overlooking the Tiese Valley, it fairly flaunts its antiquity and its village street is a tiny remnant of Tudor England.

By contrast, the village sign is almost starkly simple: a roadside silhouette of the church lychgate flanked by two of the famous clipped yew trees that form the approach to the church door.

When it was still deep in the primaeval Andredsweald forest, Brenchley became a centre of the Wealden iron industry that once made this part of the industrial heartland of England. After the foundries closed during the 18th century, however, the village settled down to become the very model of the Garden of England image, to which clouds of orchard blossom contributed handsomely every spring.

All Saints Church was founded in about 1170 as a chapel of Yalding church and was given to Tonbridge Priory, together with the manor, by Richard de Clare of Tonbridge Castle, although the present sandstone church was not built until 1233.

The house known as Wat Tyler's is a 15th century timber-framed building on Castle Hill. The Old Workhouse is one of the architectural gems of Brenchley, as are the 14th century Old Vicarage and 15th century Old Palace, once the home of the Duke of St Albans, son of Nell Gwynn and Charles II. Brenchley Manor is generally regarded as one of the finest Tudor houses in Kent.

Today, Brenchley is in the same parish as its larger neighbour, Matfield.

BRIDGE

The village sign at Bridge, near Canterbury, is a simple wooden cut-out of the steepled church behind a two-arched bridge over a representational river, all surmounting the name of the village in clear white lettering on a blue ground. It says it all, with unpretentious clarity.

The village takes its name from the series of bridges across the Little Stour, also known as the Nailbourne, and the most prominent building is the church, which retains Norman details among its much restored fabric.

A celebrated resident was Count Louis Zborowski, the racing car driver, who inherited Bridge Hill House and a multi-million pound fortune in 1911 enabling him to indulge his passion for fast cars. He and his brother, Len, built the famous aero-engined Chitty-Chitty-Bang-Bang cars, made even more famous by the film that revived the name.

A parallel enthusiasm for miniature railways led him to build one, in partnership with Capt John Howey, which became a fore-runner of the famous Romney Marsh "Little Railway", although that was not built until after his death in 1924 aged 29 while competing in the Italian Grand Prix at Monza in a supercharged Mercedes which left the track and hit a tree.

It echoed his own father's death, which happened near Nice in 1903 when his Mercedes hit a wall during a hill climb competition.

BROOMFIELD

The village sign at Broomfield is one of a number of Kent signs made by Bernard Hill of Coxheath: a bold, eye-catching design in a boxed wooden frame surmounted by the county badge.

The name of the village is in bold black lettering on a green label across the top and the main feature of the design is a gold coloured church bell, a reminder that it was on the Broomfield-Ulcombe border that the famous Kentish bellfounder Joseph Hatch had his home, in a house now called Roses Manor Farm, also featured on the sign. Some of his bells were probably cast in neighbouring KingSwood and others would have been cast nearby the churches in which they were to be hung.

Hatch died in 1636, by which time more than 200 of his bells hung in Kent churches and in Canterbury Cathedral. Many are still ringing, and there is a detailed account of Hatch and his bells inside Broomfield church.

Broomfield was mentioned in the Domesday Survey in 1086 and for centuries the village was part of the Leeds Castle estate. Several owners of the castle, which is nearby, were buried there, including members of the Fairfax family, the last of whose line, Lord Robert, died in 1793. In the 1950s, during the ownership of Olive, Lady Baillie, a complete programme of modernisation of all the houses was carried out. Today, only part of the village is still castle property, including Barrack Cottages, which were once billets for soldiers during the Napoleonic Wars.

The sign stands on the village green, beside the approach to the church and close by St Margaret's Well, which is identified by a wooden cross and which is believed to have been on record since 1607.

CHART SUTTON

This is one of those two-sided signs, differently illustrated on each face. On one side is a simple, stylised representation of the church in flames, and the dates 1782 and 1982. It recalls that the church, St Michael's, was virtually totally destroyed by fire in 1779, leaving only the 14th century tower, and was rebuilt, entirely with money raised by public subscription, by 1782, 200 years before the sign was erected. The fire was apparently started when lightning struck the building and the heat was so intense that it melted the bells in the tower.

New bells were cast and hung, though not, it seems by the local bellfounder, Stephen Norton, who built Norton Court and may have been casting bells locally in the latter half of the 14th century.

The other side of the sign shows that recurring image on signs in Kent: two round oast kilns and a sprig of hops, and inset in the bottom right-hand corner is a shield bearing the county emblem, the White Horse on a red ground.

Chart Sutton is one of the Three Suttons, the other two being Sutton Valence and East Sutton. Its name is said to derive from the description of a south farmstead in open country. In fact, the parish today forms a strip of land running north-south down a hillside, with the northern end on the ridge and the southern in the Weald.

COLLIER STREET

In naming the 360 or so villages scattered throughout Kent, Collier Street would probably not be one that would come readily to mind. It is even overlooked by most of the county's guide books.

Yet, although it is little more than a few houses along each side of the B2162 south of Yalding, it has a church and a school and - what many much larger villages do not have - its own village sign.

It stands at the roadside near the church, a simple rectangle, in a metal frame decorated with wrought ironwork, on which is painted a stylised rural scene with a church spire flanked by a pair of round oast kilns rising above a foreground of billowy greenery. The name of the village is prettily lettered across the bottom.

That name is said to refer to the family of William Colier which was prominent during the 14th century. During the hop farming boom of the 19th and early 20th centuries, Collier Street shared the complete change of character imposed by the annual migration of thousands of Cockney hop-pickers to the Weald. It was a major event - often, THE major event - of each year and it was anticipated with almost equal measures of eagerness and trepidation.

Hops are no longer a mainstay of the local economy, but the oast kilns that feature on so many village signs bear witness to the affection with which their heyday is still remembered.

COOLING

The very small and somewhat remote village of Cooling on the Hoo Peninsular has an impressive box-framed sign full of descriptive features and, most unusually, topped with the Royal arms.

It is a colourful sign, illustrated with a representation of old St James' Church, closed since 1976 and declared redundant in 1979 but still well-maintained and open to visitors. The sign also includes a reference to the churchyard group of 13 graves of members of the Comport family that died out en masse in the 1770s and which Charles Dickens borrowed for the "five little stone lozenges" marking the graves of Pip's brothers in Great Expectations.

The author himself looks at the church from an adjoining portrait and the centrepiece of the sign is the towered gateway of 14th century Cooling Castle. The house became a "castle" after it was fortified by Sir John Cobham and it was then that the gateway was built. The house was later owned by Sir John Oldcastle, a leading Lollard who escaped arrest by the Archbishop of Canterbury but was eventually caught, tried, hanged and then burned outside St Giles' Hospital in London on Christmas Day 1417.

Below the great gateway, which is sadly less complete than the sign suggests, water-fowl are a reminder that Cooling is on the edge of the extensive marshlands on the seaward side of the village, where the peninsular becomes a fist of land punching the estuary of the rivers Thames and Medway which flank it.

COXHEATH

Until 1756, Coxheath was one of the last true wildernesses left in Kent, a place known best to smugglers and highwaymen. But with the start of the Seven Years' War, it became a military camp and a source of conflict between the military and civil authorities about who should punish soldiers who misbehaved in the confines of nearby Maidstone.

After the Battle of Waterloo and the defeat of Napoleon in 1815 the camp was closed and the village began to grow around the former officers' quarters and other permanent buildings on the site.

When England expected Napoleon to attempt an invasion, Coxheath was part of the network of warning beacons set up to alert the country to the imminent arrival of the French and all this history is commemorated in the village sign which swings from a metal bracket fixed to a timber upright topped by an empty beacon basket. It stands beside the main road through the village and its size and height above ground make it difficult to decipher all its features, which include twin shields, one bearing three tents above crossed guns (the military connection) and the other representing the fruit growing character of the surrounding countryside.

Above them, the Latin motto "Pagus Noster, Domus Nostra" translates as "Our Village, Our Home" and linking the two shields is the Kent White Horse badge. The name of the village is enscrolled across the bottom of the sign.

The design was by Bernard Hill as a result of a competition organised by Coxheath Parish Council in 1971.

CRANBROOK

There is an unpretentious simplicity about the Cranbrook village sign, which features a crane (the bird) standing elegantly on one leg in a stylised brook, with bullrushes in the background. The name of the village underlines the square-framed picture in plain bold lettering above the solid-looking capital that tops the timber upright.

What more is needed to announce a village whose name is generally said to have derived from the Crane brook which runs through it, or possibly from the Old English word 'cranbroc', meaning 'marshy ground frequented by cranes'?

However it earned its name, Cranbrook was once the undisputed capital of the Weald in Kent. The author H E Bates (author of The Darling Buds of May) once wrote that Cranbrook gave the impression of a town trying to remember what once made it important.

If the village itself cannot remember, history can. Cranbrook rose to importance in the days when it was the centre of the Wealden woollen and iron industries and the largest and only really industrial town in Kent, bigger than either Canterbury or Maidstone at that time.

Today it hovers a little uncertainly between large village and small town, identified more thrustingly than by its village sign by the towering landmark that is the 75ft high Union Mill and by nearby St Dunstan's Church, which is still sometimes known as the Cathedral of the Weald.

CURTISDEN GREEN

It would be possible to quibble with the description of the little community here as a village at all and, in fact, it is part of the parish of Goudhurst, just off the B2079 a couple of miles north of Goudhurst itself.

But it certainly has its own village sign, on the green opposite Bethany School Chapel. The fretted iron frame silhouettes an oast house and a tree, with the name and the date, 2000, in white lettering underneath.

A metal plate on the timber upright to which the sign is bracketed acknowledges the generous help of Goudhurst Parish Council and Bethany School to local residents in providing the sign to celebrate the millennium.

Bethany School began as Bethany House, which was built by Joseph Kendon in 1865. There, he taught boys who paid 2d (less than 1p) a week for tuition. He was also a pioneer of social work among the London hop-pickers who migrated to the Wealden hop farms where, throughout much of the second half of the 19th century, the conditions in which they lived and worked were still very poor indeed. He was an evangelistic member of the Plymouth Brethren and he popularised his missionary work among the Londoners by offering free teas to those who attended his prayer meetings.

The school later developed into a major private boarding school for boys although it was not until 1993 that the first girls were admitted as pupils.

DETLING

Most village signs are supported on posts but the handsome millennium sign at Detling is of sculpted stone with brick wings topped with metal railings and with a seating area.

It stands opposite St Martin's churchyard, in Church Lane: an eight foot high column of Portland Stone which spells out the name of the village. A robust-looking cockerel that emerges from the "D" at the top, is a reference to the Cock Horse (formerly The Cock) Inn. Other symbolism incorporated into the column includes a shell, the badge adopted by pilgrims and a reminder that the Pilgrims' Way crosses the parish. The brick wings terminate in brick pillars, one topped by a badger and the other by a woodpecker, examples of the local wildlife.

Carved into the stone are date panels, MM (Roman 2000) and AD 2000, and two other panels, one of which reads: "This work was made possible by various donations from people of this parish and the Arts Council of England. Sculptor S Buchanan" (in fact, Simon Buchanan, a young Surrey artist). The other panel acknowledges the financial support for the £20,000 cost of the project that was received from Kent Rural Action, Kent Agricultural Society (owners of the County Showground at Detling), Maidstone Borough Council and Detling Parish Council. That support included a National Lottery grant of £13,000.

It took the village about four years to bring this ambitious project to fruition but it has put Detling on the village signs map in a big way.

DITTON

Ditton's sign was unveiled, as the plaque on the supporting cross beam records, on November 3, 1996 by M Jose Collette, Mayor of Rang-du-Fliers, Ditton's French twin town, and Mr John Day, Chairman of Ditton Parish Council.

Unusually shaped, with a scalloped top, it depicts Ditton's St Peter's Church in a sylvan setting, with the stream, which is a village feature, and water fowl. The prominent name DITTON on a scrolled label surmounts a garland of flowers, fruit and hops illustrative of the character of the neighbourhood.

Above the picture a quartered roundel repeats the church, water fowl and trees and includes the clasped hands of friendship, surrounded by the words DITTON PARISH KENT.

The overall decorativeness of the sign is emphasized with scrolled wrought iron brackets supporting the metal half-frame and with shaped timber supports connecting the cross beam with the main timber upright.

The sign stands on its timber upright in a little triangle of green beside the A20, at its junction with Station Road (leading to Aylesford). On the opposite side of the A20, where Ditton's war memorial stands, is New Road, which leads directly into the village and past the church and its neighbouring stream.

DODDINGTON

Doddington, in the Newnham Valley between Faversham and Sittingbourne, was one of several Kent villages that celebrated the new millennium with a new village sign: a very distinctive wrought iron double oval with a diamond centre instead of the more usual rectangle, with elegantly scrolled supports springing from its timber upright.

The name of the village and the date, 2000, fill the top and bottom of the double oval and the centrepiece is a fruit tree. A left-hand segment at the top depicts a swallow and acorns; the right-hand is filled with strawberries and cherries. In the bottom half is a chequers board, an allusion to the 12th century (although altered since then) village pub, The Chequers, and a representation of the church which is dedicated to the Decollation (beheading) of St John the Baptist.

The story goes that Richard I (the Lionheart) spent a night in Doddington on his way back to London from a Crusade. He had with him a souvenir, the stone on which John the Baptist was beheaded, and that inspired the unique dedication of the local church.

It was not the only Royal visit. Edward I and his Queen Eleanor stayed there for several days in 1304.

More recently, in the early years of the 20th century, Dr Josiah Oldfield, author and penal reformer, came to live in Doddington where he was co-founder, with India's Mahatma Gandhi, of the Fruitarian Society, which they formed to promote vegetarian eating.

EAST FARLEIGH

Most Kent villages content themselves with one identifying sign, usually at a main road entrance into the village or else in the village centre. East Farleigh, however, has four.

It is a somewhat scattered community with its barely discernible centre at the road junction flanked by The Bull public house and St Mary's church. There, a somewhat plain sign, without decorative ironwork, stands between two trees, an old stone mounting block and a drinking trough.

The sign itself features a representation of the five-arched East Farleigh bridge, with wavy lines to illustrate the River Medway beneath it. The bridge is reckoned to be one of the best examples of its mediaeval period in southern England. Parliamentarian troops under the command of Lord Fairfax who crossed the bridge on their way to subdue Royalist forces in Maidstone in 1648 would have found it an easier crossing point than today's motorists for whom a very sharp bend at one end and a railway level crossing at the other pose problems and cause delays.

Above the bridge, the sign shows three cowled round oast kilns flanked by foliage. The kilns are a reminder that the steep hillside that climbs up from the River Medway were once, not so very long ago, clothed with hop gardens.

EAST MALLING

East Malling's village sign was designed by parish councillor Paul Stroud for East Malling Conservation Group and erected in the early 1990s. Starting from the top left of its relatively small, iron-framed rectangle, it depicts the church of St James the Great beside one of the six water mills once powered by the stream which, on the sign, flows past timbered Mouse Cottage, representing the village's many attractive old houses. The house is part-framed by a sprig of hops, a reminder that this was part of the Mid Kent hop growing region until the mid-20th century.

The symbolic stream then bends geometrically to frame an heraldic shield, a reference to the Twisdens of Bradbourne House, one of the finest Queen Anne houses in England and now the headquarters of Horticultural Research International, formerly and still better-known as East Malling Research Station, represented by two fruit trees. The stream runs out through a gap in the ragstone wall frame on its way to join the River Medway.

The name of the village stands out in bold gold-coloured lettering across the bottom of the sign, which is suspended within a black metal frame topped with decorative ironwork and supported on scrolled metal brackets.

Although smaller, East Malling is older than neighbouring West Malling. King Egbert, sometimes identified as the first King of the English, gave land for a church to be built there in 827.

EAST PECKHAM

There is an attractive simplicity about East Peckham's village sign, which stands in its own little shrubbery outside the village Methodist Church in The Pound. The solid, domed timber frame, decorated with wrought ironwork, encloses a metal silhouette design depicting the old hill-top St Michael's church and two round oast kilns. Seen against a plain sky background, it has an unusual air of dignity.

A metal plate on the great timber upright tells anyone who cares to read the weathered lettering that the sign was presented by East Peckham Women's Institute on the 19th May 1984.

The 18th century Kent historian Edward Hasted recorded that the stiff clay soil hereabouts "bred and fattened some of the biggest beasts in any of these parts" and, later, that same soil made this a centre of the county's hop-growing industry. The former Whitbread hop farm at nearby Beltring boasts the largest group of massed oast kilns in the world and remains a major landmark although now it is a museum and leisure centre and venue for various large-scale events throughout the year.

A century ago, East Peckham was just one of nine separate hamlets that shared St Michael's church, which has been isolated and made redundant on its hilltop relatively far from the present village which emerged during the 20th century after builders developed the existing community around The Pound as the site for the village that we have today.

EASTCHURCH

English aviation began at Eastchurch, on the Isle of Sheppey, and the village sign commemorates the fact. It features prominently an early aircraft which looks as if it is about to crash into the white building over which it is flying. The name of the village is in gold lettering on a ribbon across the bottom.

It was at Eastchurch that the young Winston Churchill learned to fly; where Charles Stewart Rolls (of the famous Rolls-Royce motor-car duo) made the first two-mile flight round the church tower and back again and, later, who made the first there-and-back cross-Channel flight. Another famous Eastchurch pioneer was Lord Brabazon of Tara, who became the holder of Pilot's Licence No 1.

The sign stands on a grass verge beside the approach road into the village, in a small flower bed in which also stands the plain roadside sign common to all villages, with just the county badge above the name.

Britain's first aircraft factory was built on 4,000 acres of Sheppey marshland by Short Brothers before they moved to Rochester.

Long before aero-engines disturbed the local peace, however, Shurland Hall was the 12th century home of the local big noise of his time, Sir Robert de Shurland, who became the principal character in the Rev Richard Barham's Ingoldsby Legend of Grey Dolphin, the knight's horse whose faithful service was rewarded with a fatal sword stroke and, in fulfilment of a prophecy, became the posthumous cause of his ungrateful master's death.

EYNSFORD

This unusually ornate timber-framed sign stands beside the A225 through the village, just south of the A20 at Farningham and its painted illustration shows the church (St Martin's) and the bridge over the River Darent. The timber upright makes a convenient place to display plaques commemorating village successes in the county's annual Best Kent Village and other competitions.

Although the river is the Darent, it flows through the Darenth Valley and it is crossed at Eynsford by both a bridge and a ford which lead out of the village centre past the distinctively barrel-roofed Old Mill towards the 16th century Plough Inn.

Unlike the remains of the Norman castle, nearby Lullingstone Castle never was a castle but was originally Lullingstone House, built in the 16th century, although only the Gatehouse and some fragments of that original building survived extensive alterations made during the 18th century specially for the benefit of a visit by Queen Anne.

The house is not open to the public but there is public access to the 600 acre park and the unique little church of St Botolph, known as The Church on the Lawn, all that remains now of the hamlet of which it was once the centre and which grew up where Romans built a villa, the foundations and some of the mosaic flooring of which have been excavated and now form part of a permanent covered display by English Heritage.

FIVE OAK GREEN

Today, Five Oak Green is a rather pleasant little residential community to the east of Tonbridge and not far from Paddock Wood. It has very little to say for itself now but in the first half of the last century it was in the heart of the Wealden hop-growing country and every year during the late summer season surrounding farms were a destination for hundreds of London hop-pickers.

A major landmark still is the Richard Wilson Holiday Home, founded at the end of the 19th century by Fr Wilson, a Stepney priest, as The Little Hoppers' Hospital. Fr Wilson regularly followed his flock from London to Kent and was disturbed by the conditions in which the hop-pickers lived during their month-long stay.

On one occasion he encountered a woman setting out to walk back to London, carrying a brown paper parcel. When asked what was in the parcel, she said it was her baby, who had died, and the priest was so moved that he founded the hospital in the bowling alley behind one of the local pubs, where sick children could be treated in the hope that such tragedies could be prevented in future.

The Five Oak Green village sign is an unpretentious framed rectangle depicting five oak leaves and a single acorn against a symbolic white cloud on a sky blue ground, with the name in clear dark-on-light brown lettering across the bottom. The frame is surmounted by relatively extravagant scrolled ironwork with a central column topped by a single acorn.

FRITTENDON

Frittenden lies between two of the main north-south routes from Maidstone through The Weald, the A229 and the A274, roughly half-way between Staplehurst and Sissinghurst.

Its most prominent building is the memorably named Bell and Jorrocks public house which is overlooked from its hillside site opposite by the village sign.

It is a pictorial sign dominated by the spire-mounted tower of the church, which is flanked by twin oast cowls and a tall chimney. In the foreground is a row of trees, fields with sheep and an owl in flight, all painted on a bell-shaped ground surrounded by oak trees. The name is enscrolled across the bottom in bold black lettering. The whole sign is box-framed in timber and surmounted with the Kent badge.

The tall chimney is a reference to the local brickmaking and the bell-shaped background acknowledges the local importance of the inn, which was once simply The Bell. When Thomas Idenden died in 1566, he left money for the trustees of the charity he endowed to have an annual meal at his expense at The Bell Inn.

Armchair tourists could be forgiven if they had never heard of Frittenden and no doubt the villagers today are just as contented to have been overlooked by pretty well all the writers of the county guide books as were their ancestors in the 11th century when William the Conqueror's Domesday bureaucrats passed it by without a mention, although we know it was there as early as 804AD, when it was named as Friddingden.

GOLDEN GREEN

Golden Green is a very small community, south of Hadlow, at a junction of the network of minor roads between the A26 Tonbridge-Maidstone road and the B2015, which passes the Beltring Hop Farm. A wayfarer would be more likely to find it by accident than by design which, no doubt, is exactly as the villagers would wish it to be.

Its village sign rises out of a triangle of grass at the southern end of the village: a rather modest, domed metalwork silhouette of oast kilns and a group of houses beneath a sunburst canopy. With a clear blue sky behind it, it has an air of shyness, as though it is a little embarrassed to be perched so high on such an improportionately substantial timber upright, which would have supported something much grander.

Although Golden Green is predominantly agricultural in character, for many years the Crystalate Works was a major local employer. The factory was an offshoot of the parent factory at Tonbridge, a pioneer of the plastics industry, whose products included the old 78 rpm gramophone records, radio and other electrical components, toys and billiard balls. The manager of the Golden Green factory was George Davis, whose house, The Pines, had a room in which his two nephews, Joe and Fred Davis, came to try out the billiard balls. They became world billiards and snooker champions. After the factory closed, the site became a housing estate.

GOUDHURST

The present village sign at Goudhurst was designed by Bridget Hayward of Curtisden Green as her entry in a competition organised as a village contribution to the Festival of Britain in 1951. It was made by a local blacksmith at Hope Mill forge, and erected by him on The Plain, beside the pond at the lower end of the main street through the village.

The fretted ironwork includes a design of fruit and hops with the county White Horse emblem in a sunburst above the name of the village, and a twin-cowled oast house below it. The whole is framed by decorative ironwork which blends attractively with the background of trees against which it stands.

Like most other "dens" and "hursts" of the Weald, Goudhurst began as a clearing in the primaeval Andredsweald forest and when the Domesday bureaucrats were compiling their record of the Conqueror's realm in 1086, it was not deemed worthy of mention, although we know there was a settlement by then.

It belonged to the manor of Chilham and the Star and Eagle public house was once a monastic building neighbouring St Mary's church.

Goudhurst was the home of the Kingsmill brothers, leading lights in the notorious Hawkhurst Gang of smugglers, and it was around the church that villagers confronted and defeated the gang in what became known as the Battle of Goudhurst in 1747.

GRAFTY GREEN

Grafty Green is a very small village just south of Boughton Malherbe and in the parish of that name, which is why the rather handsome timber frame of the village sign bears both names, one above and one below the pictorial sign within the frame.

The picture depicts the Y-fork of the roads round the small fenced area of village green, illustrative of the name, Grafty Green, which describes an area of enclosed grass. One of the two roads goes right towards Boughton Malherbe, the other snaking towards Platt's Heath.

In the foreground is a field gate with the millennium date, MM, on it and on the green is the very handsome silver birch that was planted to commemorate the Silver Jubilee of George V (1935). Behind the green is the village pub, The King's Head, and other features of the sylvan scene include an oast house and a bailed cricket wicket, bat and ball, reminders that Boughton Malherbe Place was the home of Galfredus Mann, who was known as King of Cricket and who is remembered, among other reasons, for promoting a game of cricket on horseback in 1800.

Boughton Malherbe's St Nicholas' Church stands on the skyline, easily the oldest building in the parish. Both the manor and the church were mentioned in the Domesday Survey and it was here that Mildred Norrington, who became known as the Pythoness of Westwell, was tried in 1574, accused of witchcraft. She demonstrated that her "demonic possessions" were faked.

HADLOW

A former owner of Hadlow Castle, Walter Barton May, bequeathed the village one of the most readily recognized landmarks in Kent and the main feature of the village sign.

Hadlow Castle (never a castle, of course) was a handsome stately home begun in the 1780s on the site of an earlier house, and completed during succeeding decades. It was regarded as a somewhat eccentric pile by many people and William Cobbett, during one of his Rural Rides in 1823, described it as "an immense house stuck all over with a parcel of chimneys or things like chimneys ... with a sort of caps on them at the top to catch the earwigs."

The tower was designed by George Ledwell Taylor, who was also responsible for work at Sheerness and Chatham dockyards and some of the best parts of the West End of London. It was modelled on the tower of Fonthill Abbey in Wiltshire which in turn was inspired by a tower in Portugal. The Fonthill tower fell down in 1825 but, although truncated for safety reasons, the Hadlow Castle tower, sometimes known as May's Folly, still stands and is now a protected building. One local legend has it that Walter Barton May built it so that he could keep an eye on his wife after she left him and went home to mother at nearby Fish Hall.

He died in 1853 and was buried in Hadlow churchyard and the main part of Hadlow Castle has since been demolished.

HALLING

Halling is one of those once wholly agricultural villages to which the cement industry brought a new prosperity in the late 19th century, when it's riverside industries could be served by the sailing barges that were the juggernauts of their day.

The village sign, which depicts a red-sailed barge alongside a ruined gateway, is a reminder of those days. It is an eye-catching sign, with the illustrative medallion set into an oval of decorative ironwork containing the words Halling Parish, all inside a double rectangular iron frame topped with wrought iron scrollwork.

Since the opening of the Snodland and Halling bypass, the village is relatively traffic-free but once the Halling-Wouldham Medway ferry crossing would have been used by pilgrims travelling to and from Canterbury. In 1941 a temporary three-span military bridge was built across the river but, despite the pleas of farmers, businesses and others who found it a very convenient short cut, it was demolished in 1946 partly, it was said, because it was too low for river traffic to be able to pass under it.

Gundulph, Bishop of Rochester, who was responsible for much of the Norman architecture that remains in the diocese today, built a palace at Halling in 1077, between the church and the river, and several later bishops lived and died there. Later, it became the home of William Lambarde, who is credited with having written the first English county guide book and who lived there until 1598.

The palace survived into the 19th century as a farmhouse until it was demolished to make way for the cement works built on the site.

HARRIETSHAM

The old Pilgrims' Way crosses Harrietsham and the village sign celebrates this with a relief picture of a mediaeval pedestrian pilgrim leading a donkey carrying (presumably) his wife past a red-roofed water mill along the ancient route to Canterbury. The name of the village is inscribed in Old English characters across the top of the picture.

It is a robust-looking sign, stoutly box-framed with wrought iron scrolled brackets and other iron work.

The pictured mill would have been one of many along the Len stream which still flows in front of a row of cottages and under West Street. On the opposite side of the A20 which cuts the village in two, a terrace of almshouses perpetuates the name of local man Mark Quested, who built them in 1642. He was a member of the City of London's Fishmongers' Company, which paid for the rebuilding of the almshouses in 1770.

The Pilgrims' Way passes close by the church of St John the Baptist, a little aloof from the village, and Roman urns and Saxon coins have both been found in the parish, evidence of the antiquity of the settlement which came into the ownership of William Stede in 1579. The Stede family were the most prominent local landowners for 200 years and William's Stede House still stands, although it has had a number of different names and owners in the intervening years.

HAWKHURST

This sign, which stands on The Moor, is relatively ornately framed in scrolled wrought iron, with a picture of a hawk in flight over trees and the name of the village, in very modestly sized lettering, across the top.

This is the oldest of the two distinct parts of Hawkhurst village, half a mile south of the central point where the A268 road to Rye crosses the A229 Maidstone-Hastings road. The other part is Highgate, where the 19th century colonnaded parade of shops that flanks the A268 is probably better-known to travellers through the High Weald.

The combination of white weatherboarding and warm-coloured clay tiles that is so characteristic of this part of Kent is everywhere in Hawkhurst. Until a Second World War V1 flying bomb (doodlebug) blew it out, a stained glass window in St Laurence's Church was a memorial to the astronomer Sir John Herschel, who lived in the village from 1840 until he died in 1871. He mapped the stars of the Northern Hemisphere and founded an observatory at the Cape of Good Hope to do the same for the Southern Hemisphere. He was a President of the Royal Society and was Master of the Mint from 1850-55.

The village also lent its name to the notorious 18th century Hawkhurst Gang of smugglers and several local buildings and inns claim links with the gang.

HEADCORN

A discreet plaque on the upright beam of the Headcorn village sign explains that it was erected by the parishioners and unveiled by the Rt Hon Lord Cornwallis, Lord Lieutenant of Kent, in Festival of Britain year, 1951 in commemoration of the gift of Day's Green, on the edge of which it stands, to the parish by Alfred Day, OBE, JP.

The sign itself is slightly unusual in that, instead of the more common square frame, this one is arched. It stands on a rectangular label bearing the painted name of the village, the whole supported on carved scrolled timber brackets on either side of an inset White Horse of Kent on a red ground. Within the frame, the painted sign features a white windmill in a sylvan scene.

Tradition claims that when Queen Elizabeth I arrived there during her Progress through Kent in 1573, it was called Hedecron, probably a derivation of a Saxon original. But the Queen was so impressed by the richness of the corn growing locally that she joked it should be called "not Hedecron but Headcorn". The royal jest was taken seriously and - if legend is to be believed (and, of course, it often is not!). - that was how the village got the name by which it has been known for 400 years.

The once famous Headcorn oak tree in the churchyard finally succumbed to extreme old age but before it was axed one of its acorns was planted nearby and promises to be a worthy ancestor.

HIGH HALSTOW

One of the largest and oldest of the villages on the Hoo Peninsula, which separates the Rivers Thames and Medway before they empty into the estuary, High Halstow has no fewer than three different village signs.

One, which sits on top of a wooden signpost, helpfully identified as two and a quarter miles from Hoo, two miles from Cooling and seven miles from Grain, was provided by the local Women's Institute in 1982, its 25th year and as well as recording this information in wrought iron, together with the name of the village, it features a heron, a reference to the local Northward Hill nature reserve and heronry.

In 1996, however, the village treated itself to a new two-sided sign, created in colourful mosaic discs, one on each side of a purpose-built wall in front of the medical centre. Only one side has the name of the village, picked out in red among representations of the local road layout and wildlife. The other side has date, 1996, among representations of local features, including a heron for the heronry.

The letters HH in white inside a quartered medallion in the centre of the sign and the date, 1996, among representations of local features, including a heron for the heronry.

From the modest prominence that justifies its name, High Halstow enjoys probably the greatest variety of scenery of any village on the peninsula. There has been a church certainly since the 14th century but it and the Red Dog inn are pretty much the only remaining evidence of antiquity and the village is still growing today.

HOLLINGBOURNE

One of the most handsome of Kent's village signs is that which stands on Eyhorne Green at Hollingbourne.

Erected in 1994 by the parish council to commemorate the council's establishment in 1884, it was designed by the late Mr Jack Garnham-Wright, former parish council chairman, carved by Mark Jones of Bethersden and unveiled by descendents of original members of the council.

The unpainted sign is carved in oak in the shape of a shield surmounted by the crest of the Culpeper family which was prominent in Kent throughout the 16th, 17th and 18th centuries, and with the name of the village curving round the bottom.

The shield is divided vertically by a representation of the stream that flows through the village and horizontally by a symbolic Pilgrims' Way. The top left-hand quarter has a water mill and below that is a group of oast houses, recalling the former dominant local industries. Opposite them, occupying the whole of the right-hand side of the shield, is Hollingbourne church tower. The whole is embellished with sprays of apples, nuts, hop bine and hawthorn leaves - the name Eyhorne is said to be derived from Old English meaning a meeting place identified by a hawthorn tree.

Eyhorne Manor existed in 975 when it was responsible for the maintenance of one of the piers of Rochester Bridge but no-one knows quite how long people have lived in Hollingbourne. Stone and Bronze Age implements have been found locally and there is a tradition that the first Saxons built a fortified camp there in the fifth century AD, although all traces of that are now lost.

HIGHAM

Standing prominently at the side of the A226 Rochester-Gravesend road, Higham's sign declares the village pride in having been the home of Charles Dickens from 1857 until he died in 1870.

It is a relatively stark village sign, compared with many more colourful ones of other villages, and features a somewhat severe portrait of the author himself, flanked by the two dates of his birth and death. To make sure there is no doubt about who is pictured, his name is written above his head and below, in larger letters, is the name of the village. The frame, though, is edged with almost lacy iron scrollwork which is repeated in the brackets that support it on the timber upright.

As a small boy, out walking with his father, young Charles had admired Gads Hill House but it was not until 1857, when he was a successful 45 year-old author, that he was able to buy it from another author, Eliza Lynn Linton. Her father, the former rector, had lived there but he had just died and left the house to her. She wanted to sell it and Dickens snapped it up.

It was there that he wrote Great Expectations and Our Mutual Friend and he was working on The Mystery of Edwin Drood there when he died in 1870, leaving his last novel unfinished.

HOO ST WERBURGH

An almost lacy delicacy of wrought ironwork surrounds the central oval medallion on which is painted an armorial horse, half white and half gold, facing a fish-tailed creature. Between the two is the church and the sails of a barge on the river behind it, with the date 1894 among trees above both. Below is a ribbon on which is written Hoo St Werburgh Parish Council. The name of the village is spelled out in iron lettering above and below the medallion.

It stands behind a stone horse trough used as a flower container and a plaque explains: "This village sign has been erected to commemorate the centenary of Hoo St Werburg Parish Council, 1895-1995".

The village identifies itself among other Hoo Peninsula villages by taking the name of its church, which it did formally as recently as 1968. Before that, local people simply called it Hoo, and many still do. It is bypassed now by the A228 spine road but it remains the principal village of the Hundred of Hoo. The oldest parts of the church are 13th century and its dedication is to the daughter of Wulfhere, 7th century King of Mercia who founded a nunnery for her here. She was revered because, when geese flew in and ravaged crops, she called the birds to her and explained the problem, after which they never attacked the villagers' crops again. Local lore has a long memory for that sort of thing!

HUNTON

Every village sign is unique, but some are undeniably more memorable than most.

Like Hunton's "stained glass window" sign, which is composed of a mosaic of geometric shapes creating an illustration, the central foreground of which is dominated by a fruit tree, with the spire of St Mary's parish church thrusting skywards behind it. The rural character of the village is symbolised by a pattern of fields and a sheep which looks out of the picture in one bottom corner, while a cricket wicket in the other pays tribute to the local cricket club.

The name of the village is spelled out in bold lettering across the bottom and the rectangular sign is bordered with representations of fruit and other local crops, with a pair of swimming ducks acknowledging that the River Beult flows through the parish on its way to join the River Medway at Yalding.

The sign, which was commissioned by the parish council in 1994, was designed and executed by artist Peter Street.

Hunton is one of those villages with little to say for itself now, although 18th century Hunton Court, next to the church, was once the home of Liberal Prime Minister (1908-15) Sir Henry Campbell-Bannerman and the church is essentially 13th century, with more recent additions.

IDEN GREEN

To find Iden Green, it is necessary to travel the old Roman road between the B2086 through Benenden and the A268 through Sandhurst. The village clusters very modestly indeed around a road junction and the village sign stands at the roadside, hard against a hedge that seems to be doing its best to obscure it.

There is an honest rusticity about the sign's robust wooden frame, supported by unembellished wooden brackets on the support post, with an almost apologetic afterthought of ornamentation provided by the wrought ironwork that crowns the whole.

The illustration, as the plate on the upright explains, depicts the yew pasture from which the name of the village is derived (Old English "iw" translating as "yew", and "den" a pasture), and the village pump which commemorated the diamond jubilee of Queen Victoria in 1897.

The same plate also tells anyone who reads it that the sign was erected to commemorate the millennium in Iden Green and was unveiled at midnight on December 31, 1999.

The village has very little to say for itself historically, although Romans certainly travelled this way. The road through the village is part of the Roman road through the Weald from Rochester to Hastings and rough stone paving blocks found in the local stream suggest that this was a fording point along the road.

INDEX